Then there was Light

Arabella Hille

Then there was Light

Printed at Stow Park Church Print Training Project U.K.
"Helping young people to have a better future".
www.stowparkchurch.org.uk

Author: Arabella Hille
Design: Arabella Hille
Photography: Arabella Hille

Published by
Arabella Hille (Australia) 2012
ABN: 96962551763

The moral right of the author has been asserted

All Rights Reserved
This book may not be reproduced in whole or in part, stored, posted on the internet or transmitted in any form or by any means, electronic, mechanical, photocopying, recording, or other, without written permission from the author.

Then there was Light 1st ed. 2012

National Library of Australia
Cataloguing-in-Publication Data:

Then there was light / Arabella Hille

ISBN: 978-1-105-95966-0 (pbk.)

A821.4

www.thentherewaslight.net

Copyright © Arabella Hille, 2012

Table of Contents

Poems

Affirmations	15
The Light	16
I Am	17
Another year	18
Joy Rising	19
Past and Present	20
Sometimes	21
Dreams	22
My Father	23
Silence	24
Drive	25
Awake	26
Life	27

The Tree	28
I Have	29
Deal Breaker	30
Integrity	31
Temptation	32
Haiku	33
The Apology	34
A year ago & A year on	35
The Beach House	36
The Storm	37
Stronger	38

Inspirational Messages

Modern Proverbs	41
Leadership	42
Your Worth	43
Who are you?	44
A Reason to live	45
Success	46
Take Action	47
Children	48
Change	49
Connect	50
Searching	51
Choose Wisely	52
Modern Wisdom	53
Success & Failure	54
With an Ear to Hear	55

Assumptions	56
Wealth	57
The Pit	58
Anger	59
Time	60
Lead	61
Believe	62
The Right to Fly	63

This book belongs to

This book is dedicated to my Mother

Introduction

Then there was Light is collection of poems and inspirational messages that are gleaned from the last three years of my life. Journey with me as we face the trials and tribulations together and learn how to move forward and be victorious! My desire is to share what i've learned in order to inspire, teach, motivate and comfort you. No matter how bad things are, or seem in your life there is a light at the end of the tunnel and you are not alone.

Arabella Hille

Poems

Affirmations

I am in control of
my emotions

I am in control of
myself

I am beautiful in
the morning

I am beautiful
at night

I am loved at
all times

even in the
darkness

The Light

The light that is in me is also in you
it resonates in everything that we do
let us unite together sister and brother
and learn how to love and cherish one another.

I Am

I am sad
I am hurt
I am lost
    I am mending
        I am forgiving
            I am finally moving...
on.

Another year

Another year
another day
in my mind I'm far away
I run through the forests and up over the trees
I lift off the ground and soar over the seas
I circle around the tall mountain peaks
hovering over the desolate streets
I see human lives pass before my eyes
so many tragedies and so many lies
I run away quickly feeling stronger
I run to where my heart can hurt no longer
I open my eyes and turn around
there you are never letting me down
I feel the breath of life upon my face
oh how I love your endless grace
your gentle kiss tells me that I am home
and now I no longer feel so alone
I am light
I am happy
and I am free
no longer in
my dreams
but in
reality

Joy Rising

I feel the love
washing over me
It comes from
the wind which
blows from the
sea
Let us
connect
together
you and
me
So our
happiness
can shine
for all to see

Past and Present

Today I am low

Yesterday life just seemed to flow

Today is too much

Yesterday I quivered at your touch

Today I cry

Yesterday I was oblivious to your lie

Today I am frustrated

Yesterday I was happy and elated

Today everything I had was taken away

Yesterday seemed just like any other day

Sometimes

Sometimes
you could be so kind
Sometimes you blew
my mind

Sometimes we would be so strong
Sometimes I am glad
that you are gone

Sometimes you held me all night
Sometimes you would
be my light

Sometimes I gazed in your eyes
Sometimes I looked
over your lies

Because sometimes I felt your love
and sometimes just
**isn't
good
enough**

Dreams

Sitting in the aftermath of war wondering what's behind the next door i feel this urge deep in my soul an inner truth trying to grab a hold realising something about myself now taking my dreams back off the shelf.

My Father

I have
been calm
and angry
<u>I have been giving and selfish</u>
I have been free
and caged
I have been open
and closed
I have been trusting
and jealous
I have been mending
and unforgiving
I have been peaceful
and boisterous
I have been joyful
and sad
I have been light
and dark
he sees my beauty in my ugliness

Silence

Silence falls all around
in your eyes it's quiet

Silence penetrates my soul
I can no longer hear your heart beat

Silence fills up time and space
now you're just an empty vessel

Silence is the gift of thought
and your last one was of me

Drive

Don't
allow
doubt
or
fear
to
place
your
life in
neutral
gear
Just
push
the
pedal
to
the
floor
and
turn
your
life
into
something
more

Awake

One morning I woke up to see that
I didn't recognise who
was looking back
at me
I washed
my
face
and washed
away my disgrace
and vowed never
to go back to that awful place

Life

Life is more than what we   see
Life is more than what we   achieve
Life is more than words   express
Life is more than life and   death
Life is more than riches or   glory

So get out there and write your story

The Tree

Listen

you will know

a tree by the fruit that it bears

it may have strong roots to support you

it may have long branches to house you

and it may have big green leaves to shade you

but if that tree bears sour fruit then that tree is

rotten you will know the right tree when it comes

along its beauty on the outside will match its

beauty

on

the

inside

I Have

I have cried enough tears to fill a lake

I have burnt myself whilst I baked

I have danced crazily in the rain

I have lost a diamond down the drain

I have laughed so hard I couldn't breathe

I have worn my heart upon my sleeve

I have been lost and I have been found

I have hit my head on the ground

I have been caged and then I was freed

I have been a victim of man's dirty greed

I have travelled and seen many places

I have forgotten oh so many faces

I have hated but then I learned to forgive

I have been happy because I have lived.

Deal Breaker

The hurt inside
won't go away
The lies you told
my love you betrayed
You cannot comprehend
the damage you've done
because all you do is
look after number one
If only you would see
through my eyes
Then maybe you
will finally realise
that the love that
I had for you was real
And you were the one
who broke this deal

Integrity

Keep yourself honest and true
your integrity is the one thing they
can't take from you

Temptation

We
aren't what
we speak
we are
what
we
do
Always
remain
honest
and
true
even
when
others
try
to
corrupt you

Haiku

Blades in motion
Breeze cool on my face
To kill heat

Peace in mind
In my most secret place
Guard it well

The sun shines
Mornings are at my place
I'm up now

Water so fresh
Clear right to the bottom
Feet on sand

The Apology

I'm sorry for the hurt your heart has
suffered
I'm sorry for all the years your voice was
muffled
I'm sorry your childhood was up and
down
I'm sorry that your were hurt when I wasn't
around
I'm sorry for all the years that were
lost
And I'm so sorry for the great
cost
I'm sorry really isn't good enough yes I
know
I'm sorry is the first seed that I hope you will let me
sow

A year ago & A year on

A year ago the doors closed on
your dreams
A year ago closure is what
it seemed
A year ago your voice fell
deadly silent
A year ago the walls put an end to
your violence
A year ago my heart was full
of compassion
A year ago I thought you were
starting to learn
your lesson

                        A year on you walk out to
                                  start again
                        A year on you try to
                                  make amends
                  A year on a year ago seems
                                  so old
                    A year on my heart has
                                grown cold
        A year on I don't see you as a man but
                                        a boy
                A year on i've finally found
                                      my joy

The Beach House

Long
white panels
old timber fading
in the sun your graceful
in age is what you've become
wooden struts that dig down into
the ground like long legs that are the
envy of town glass frontage overlooking
the sea gives me a feeling of being totally free

The Storm

The storm is all around but she stands very still. She is beaten by the wind and braces against the waves. They try to tear down what he built in her long ago. Calm on the water she is strong and underestimated. She is of the material that they wish they were. Tearing her down is their hearts sole desire. She stares down the storm in a quiet elegant manner. The waves cease to lash as the storm subsides and the little house remains as strong as ever.

Stronger

The terror you felt when your world came down
was to make you stronger not to allow you to
drown. It was to show you the way and to show you
the light that there's love in the day and no love in
the night.

Inspirational Messages

Modern Proverbs

A man in a position of power is blessed
he who abuses it is cursed

A book is not justified by its cover
it is justified by its contents

A person with wealth but no wisdom is poor
a person with wisdom gains much

Leadership

A true leader is a servant to everyone. They do not do it for themselves but for a higher purpose. They see where the road leads when others do not. They guide with truth and kindness. Whilst their love is like a gentle breeze their wrath is like a thousand fires which never cease to burn.

Your Worth

Regardless of your race, age, colour or height you are human therefore you have worth and value.

Who Are You?

You aren't who you say you are
you are what you do.

A Reason to Live

You were put upon this earth for a reason

Your life wasn't given to you for you to waste

You are made exactly how you were meant to be

Self-acceptance is the start of a peaceful existence

Success

Success shouldn't be measured by the depth of one's pocket but by the depth of one's soul.

Take Action

Your Time is now opportunities are all around you so what you do today is as important as what you do tomorrow and now is the time to take action.

Children

Your children are an extension of yourself. Treat them as you would expect them to treat others.

Change

To change your life the first step is to change the way you think.

Connect

You cannot fully connect with another until you have learned to connect with yourself.

Searching

There is light even in the darkest of places
all you need to do is find the source of it.

Choose Wisely

What you say and do to others can have a huge impact on their life. So choose what you say and do wisely because what you do to others today may just come back around to you tomorrow.

Modern Wisdom

I can't is a word fearful
people use

Wisdom is a gift and
knowledge is learnt
use both together and it
will serve you well

Assumption is another way
of saying, "I can't be bothered
to find out the truth"

Corruption is the massacre
of one's soul

Those that boast of a pure heart
often have a heart full of evil

Success & Failure

To truly appreciate your success you need to have felt what failure feels like first.

With an Ear to Hear

You can't teach until

you've learnt

Assumptions

If you actually tried rather than assuming you can't then you'll realise that you can and probably find that you are more capable than you thought.

Wealth

Your contentment and happiness
doesn't lie in another it lies within
that is where you'll find the kingdom
you've been searching for.

The Pit

<pre>
                                         out
                                      climb
                                    and
                                  above
                                from
                              ladder
              bottom of the pit find the
         the
      reached
    have
   you
 when
</pre>

Anger

Anger gives you tunnel vision
and it closes you off to solutions
that are waiting for you to find.

Time

Do not waste your time on revenge. Instead focus your time on forgiveness. This will set your soul free to receive the blessings that are waiting around the corner for you.

Lead

You cannot lead until

you have followed

Believe

If you don't believe in yourself
how can you expect others to?

The Right to Fly

You have the right to fly so do not let anyone clip your wings.

About the Author

Arabella Hille is a devoted mother, student, and avid blogger. She has been writing from a very young age and won her first poetry competition at the tender age of fifteen. Arabella has lived all over the world in countries such as, The United States, Australia and the United Kingdom. She now resides in the beautiful state of Queensland in Australia.

Then there was Light is a collection of poems and Inspirational messages that Arabella wrote and over a three year period. In this time she experienced what we all experience in life, a major break up, change of address, change of career and a change in her social circle. Arabella found herself hurt, broken, and facing raising her son alone. Arabella had a choice, allow her ex and his bad decisions to ruin and rule her life or...

FIGHT BACK!

So instead of wallowing in self pity or denying and burying her feelings, Arabella began her healing process by writing down her thoughts and feelings in a journal. As she began to write something quite remarkable and unexpected happened...

All her thoughts and feelings came out as poems and inspirational messages. Arabella didn't think much of it at that point because she had always been a creative writer and had often dreamt of becoming an author.

Over time Arabella began feeling stronger and more confident so she started studying a Bachelors degree in communication majoring in creative writing on campus. However only after one semester Arabella was faced with yet another life changing decision. Her son was a daily victim of school yard bullying and harassment. After many attempts to rectify the situation with no avail,

Arabella felt that she had no choice but to home school him in order to provide a safe and productive learning environment. This brave move meant that Arabella could no longer attend university on campus.

Instead of giving up and placing her dreams in the too hard basket she adapted and kept on fighting! Arabella enrolled full time at Open Universities Australia so she could complete her Bachelor's degree at home and hasn't looked back since!

Arabella has learnt many lessons throughout these experiences. Two of the most important ones are; resilience and how to keep on moving forward despite the obstacles in her way. Arabella's story reflects the everyday struggles that we all can face and through this she teaches us how we can all be victorious and that there is a light at the end of the tunnel.

Arabella's message to her readers is;

"You aren't who they say you are, you are what you do!"

"Keep fighting for your dreams, no matter what obstacles are in your way there is always a way around it and you can be victorious so never give up!!"

Contact

Website & Blog:
www.thentherewaslight.net

Facebook:
www.arabellahille.info

Twitter:
www.twitter.com/ArabellaHille

Email:
arabellahille@gmail.com

If you have enjoyed this book please submit your reviews or comments in the feedback tab at:
www.thentherewaslight.net

Acknowledgements

I would like to thank God, Mike Hiscox, Rev. Paula Parish-West and Ron Prosser for their generous time and support in making my dream of becoming a published author come true.

Arabella Hille